FANCY THIS

A
New England Sketch Book

by

JACK FROST

WAVERLY HOUSE

Boston · Massachusetts

PRINTED IN THE UNITED STATES OF AMERICA BY
THE NORWOOD PRESS, NORWOOD, MASS.

FANCY THIS

A New England Sketch Book

Foreword

IT is some years now since Bostonians at their breakfast tables were greeted when they opened the pages of the Boston Herald by the drawings and writings of Mr. Jack Frost—a character whom many hitherto believed to be mythical. Despite the coolness of his name these drawings with their appended explanations were warm with human interest, and soon good citizens of Massachusetts, of the type who dislike throwing things away, began collecting them in scrap-books. The collector's instinct, so prone to take undesirable forms, was laudable in this case, for the drawings, taken altogether, are a lively comment upon the present and upon the past.

From the very beginning Mr. Frost exhibited a happy ingenuity for finding odd buildings and corners in Boston and its environs, and later up and down the roads of the New England states, and in collecting the stray pieces of ephemeral history connected with them, much of which might otherwise have been forgotten. By the use of his pen, both as an artist and a writer, he revealed the unusual aspects of doorways, roofs, bridges and buildings which thousands of his public had passed daily without a thought as to their beauty or significance. He showed us once again that a native of a city or a state is often the one who knows the least about his own environment. He aroused a new interest in old landmarks, and a new realization of how much there is in Boston and elsewhere beyond the run of ordinary existence.

For those of us who have not been careful to clip his work as it appeared it is good news that our carelessness may be repaired and that a new collection of what he has seen and found is now being given a permanent place in book form.

J. P. MARQUAND.

Newburyport, Massachusetts,
July, 1938.

Jack Frost, 1938

"THE BOSTON STUMP" ARCHITECTURALLY REPRESENTS THE "CYCLE OF TIME"

IT is said that Boston, England, furnished more worthy citizens to the great work of colonizing America than any other part of England. There has always been a firm bond between that city and Boston, Massachusetts. During the Tercentenary in 1930, a committee in which Allan Forbes, banker and collector of the historic, was an active member, presented thousands of pounds to aid in the restoration of the "Old Stump" of St. Botolph's Cathedral, pictured above. It is one of England's most beautiful churches, and its tallest. It is fitting that this "Fancy This" should precede the other pictures of this book, just as pioneers from Boston, England, led in the development of America.

The Cathedral is an excellent example of Decorated and Perpendicular Gothic. Equally interesting is the fact that divisions of time are preserved architecturally in several units of the church. Uniquely enough, the winding stone staircase up the 272-foot tall tower contains 365 steps, the exact number of days in the year; the clerestory

roof is supported on just twelve stone columns, the number of months in a year; and is lighted by 52 windows, the number of weeks in the year. To further this peculiarity, it has seven doors, the number of days in a week; the stone steps in the library add to twenty-four, the sum of the hours in a day; while those ascending to the Rood Loft contain sixty, to correspond precisely with the number of minutes in an hour and number of seconds to a minute.

Boston is a word corruptly originating from "Botolph's Town" which was so called because of the wandering Saxon monk Botolph, the saint of seafaring men. Legend has it that he came to the town then called Icanhoe, Lincolnshire, England, and founded a priory about 654. He absorbed the identity of the town so completely, that as early as 1270 it was referred to as "Botolfston". Many relics and souvenirs of Old Boston exist in the newer Boston, such as gifts in Christ Church, King's Chapel, City Hall, the Public Library and other places.

"SCHOOL CHILDREN'S CLOCK" IN FANEUIL HALL MUST BE OPENED IN 1950

FANEUIL HALL, which shares the above sketch with Boston's impressive Customs House tower has played a most important role in the history of Massachusetts and this nation. The Hall was completed in 1742, the great hall over the market being called "Faneuil Hall" in honor of the donor, Peter Faneuil (1700-1743), who felt that the city badly needed a market house. The building was burned in 1761, rebuilt in 1762, and enlarged in 1805 under the supervision of the famous architect, Charles Bulfinch. The dimensions of the hall itself are 74 feet 3 inches by 75 feet 3 inches. A clock was given by the school children of Boston in 1850. Their names are to be read when a century has passed and the box, in which these "penny subscribers" are enumerated, is removed from the case. The grasshopper weathervane atop the cupola was made in 1742. In this hall the protests against the Stamp Act were voted. This and similar meetings secured for it the title "Cradle of Infant Liberty". Sorrowful occasions arose also, such as the surrendering of their arms to General Gage by Bostonians, and its use as a theatre for the entertainment of British officers. Today when the bustling, odoriferous market is the most prominent feature of the building, one needs but enter the Hall itself or that of the Ancient and Honorable Artillery Company of Massachusetts to be transported in atmosphere to those long gone days when Wendell Phillips was fighting slavery, George Washington was banqueted in the building, Samuel Adams, Robert Treat Paine, John Hancock, Rufus Choate, and other notables of the past were busy establishing the Heritage of Liberty which could be ours.

THE BIRTHPLACE OF RADCLIFFE COLLEGE

THIS quaint old house at 6 Appian Way, Cambridge, is the birthplace of Radcliffe College. When the college was founded in 1879 four rooms in this building, known as the Carret House, were used for carrying on all of the activities of the "Harvard Annex" as the college was first known. For a laboratory the early students used the bathroom. The house was rented by a committee of seven Cambridge women, who organized Radcliffe to afford women the advantages of Harvard instruction. Thirty-three Harvard professors volunteered to give classes at the new school, including LeBaron Russell Briggs who later became dean of Harvard and president of Radcliffe. In his first Greek class he met the woman he later married, Mary De Quedville. The house was used for six years when the college purchased its present administration center, 125-year-old Fay House at 10 Garden Street.

A BOSTON STREET WITH FOUR SIDEWALKS

STATE STREET not only has the fine Old State House building at its head, but owing to the position of the building in the center of the street, it has a double set of sidewalks. Two of them border the Old State House itself, and two are on the outer sides of the divided State Street. The Old State House was built in 1748 on the site of the town's earliest market place. About 1878 it served for the most part as an office building for several insurance companies, one of which, the Continental, was incorporated with a capital of $500,000 in 1852 and paid out exactly that amount for losses resulting from the Boston fire.

THE DECEPTIVE HOUSE OF QUINCY'S GREAT MAN

THE quaint little house surrounded by trees is the birthplace of John Adams, second President of the United States. The average observer would remark to himself upon the attractive "clapboard house," but not so the well-versed. For, although the house says "wood," its walls are of brick, and unique as it sounds, the clapboards have no board base, but are fastened directly to the brick with wrought iron nails; a frame house, bricked in. The house is at 129 Franklin Street, Quincy, Mass., and alongside of it is the home of John Quincy Adams, sixth President, and modelled similar to the other. Both are painted red, with white border.

MOST FAMOUS GIRLS' STORY WRITTEN HERE

ONE of the oldest houses in Concord, Mass., gained additional fame by the fact that there the most famous of all girls' stories was written. In the Orchard House, built about 1650, Louisa May Alcott created "Little Women."

Miss Alcott's room was that to the upper right of the front of the rustic appearing dwelling shown in the sketch. The "School of Philosophy," of which her father was dean, was housed in a nearby building.

The Orchard House is a mecca for admirers of the Alcott books, and is open to inspection at certain hours for their benefit. Concord preserves the tradition of the famous novelist and in 1932, when the 100th anniversary of her birth was observed, the Concord Players presented a stage version of "Little Women." At that time her publishers announced that the Alcott books had reached a total of 7,500,000 copies.

THE Boston Stone, shown in the sketch, is among the oldest and least known landmarks in the city. The "stone," a globe 20 inches in diameter, resting on an oblong block three feet long, is set into the wall of a building in Marshall street, North End, which cuts a small corner from Union to Hanover streets.

Nearly 250 years ago the globe and the oblong, then four times its present size, were used as a paint-grinder by Thomas Child, a house painter, whose home and shop occupied that site. The paint was placed in a large trough on one side of the block, and the globe was passed over it to make it fine.

After the death of Child in 1706 the property was purchased by Joseph Howe and at the suggestion of a tavern-keeper in the vicinity, Howe had the stone set up at the Hanover street corner of his house as a "place-finder" for the alehouse. No buildings were numbered in those days and the stone proved useful to generations of thirsty for 100 years.

When the old Child house was torn down 105 years ago and the present structure was built, the block was split into four sections and one of these, with the globe, was set into the wall as a souvenir of the past.

A WHARF ON TOP OF A WHARF

BUILDERS of Constitution Wharf did not have the skyscraper idea in mind when they raised this famous pier on Boston's waterfront. The harbor master explains that the wharf is really two wharves, the upper structure covering an old wharf which long and heavy use had caused to settle. The boat pictured is the Zizania, which habitually moors at one of the most noted wharves in the world.

WHEN ST. BOTOLPH CLUBMEN OFTEN PEOPLED FICTION

READING certain Boston bestsellers at the turn of the century, one might well believe that the St. Botolph club of that day was composed of distinctive, colorful, even dramatic personalities. In his "Goliath," Thomas Bailey Aldrich placed Watson and Willis, who used to play billiards at the noted old club. Characters of "The Pagans," a work by Arlo Bates, now almost forgotten, were members of the club, the home of which, located on Park Street, Boston, is sketched here. So were principals of "The Philistines," although that book gave the club the pseudonym of the St. Philippe. Craighead and Norton of Mrs. Adams's "Truth Dexter" were on the St. Botolph roster. Prominent among latter-day members was the late Philip Hale of Boston Herald critical fame.

.JACK FROST

EMERSON AND HAWTHORNE WROTE ON WINDOWS WITH A DIAMOND

ONE of the most famous ancient homes in America, the Old Manse, is not only the subject of one of the great American novels and the one-time home of both Emerson and Hawthorne, but its panes and panels still bear the writings of these great figures in American literature.

Near Lake Walden in Concord, Mass., this house, colonial to its smallest detail, has not been changed during the 178 years it has participated in the birth and growth of the nation. In the room which served as a study for Emerson and Hawthorne are inscriptions on the panes written with a diamond by both Hawthorne and his wife. "Man's Accidents are God's Purposes," states one, while another simply says, "Nathaniel Hawthorne. This is His Study. 1843." Of several others written by Emerson on a fireplace panel one reads:

"Peace to the soul of the blessed dead, honor to the ambition of the living. Apr. 1825. R. W. E."

THE LATE GEORGE APLEY WAS MARRIED HERE

KNOWN to all is the subject of J. P. Marquand's recent Pulitzer Prize winning novel "The Late George Apley". At the Arlington Street Church located at the corner of Arlington and Boylston Streets, Boston, the lovable Mr. Apley took unto himself a bride, Catharine Bosworth.

This view, the author believes would be especially dear to Mr. Apley. It shows the spire of the church as seen from the Public Garden, with the delicate, semi-silhouetted lace-work of the huge trees there serving as a natural tracery through which the historic church peeks.

Although the fact is little known, this steeple had its inspiration from an ancient church in old London, St. Martin's-in-the-Fields. The latter was designed by James Gibbs, an architect who rivaled Christopher Wrenn. Nell Gwynn, actress-favorite of Charles II, was buried here, and it is said that she left a bequest to provide a weekly entertainment for the bell ringers of St. Martin's.

The Boston version of "Nell Gwynn's Church" echoes its prototype to a great degree, although the spire of the London Church is wider at the base. Such is the similarity, however, that a Bostonian, thrust for the first time in view of St. Martin's, might believe that one of the landmarks of his home city had been transported across the Atlantic. All Souls Meeting House in Washington, D. C., also resembles the famous London edifice.

TITLE TO ST. PAUL'S CATHEDRAL DERIVED FROM AN INDIAN

RARELY indeed have Christians got help from an Indian in propagating their faith. However, it was necessary to have the indirect aid of John Wampas, one of the "original Americans," in building St. Paul's Cathedral where it stands today on Tremont Street, Boston.

Wampas held title to the northerly part of the land on which the cathedral was built. This consisted of a plot about 32 feet in frontage and 210 feet deep. Robert Wyard and his wife, Sarah, deeded the plot to the Indian by a paper dated Jan. 28, 1666, which was recorded in Suffolk registers on Sept. 28, 1668. Whether or not Wampas embraced the faith of those who eventually acquired his land is not recorded, and certainly he never visualized the fine edifice which now graces the spot.

JACK FROST
1936

ONE OF CONNECTICUT'S OLDEST HOUSES IN MASSACHUSETTS

STRANGE as it may seem, one of Connecticut's oldest houses is now situated in Massachusetts. The building shown in the sketch, which dates back 220 years, was moved last year to Decatur street, Bass Rock, from Thompson, Ct. It is owned by Edward Ingraham of 7 Lowell street, Cambridge. When the house was built, the town of Thompson was known as Killingly, Ct. It was first owned by Daniel Shapley, a weaver. Later it came into the possession of John Hichols of Kansas City, who sold it to the present owner.

It was carried to its present site in 12 truckloads, the moving being done under the supervision of Harold F Conant. The distance was 104 miles.

The front door of the house was not a part of the original Connecticut dwelling. It came from the Ballou house in Cumberland, R. I., which adjoined the birthplace of President Garfield's mother. Before the door is a stone eight feet square and weighing two and one-half tons.

TRAGIC PROPHECY OF YOUNG BIBLIOPHILE FULFILLED

THE unwitting prophesy of a young book lover, which has become famous through its association with one of the greatest marine disasters in history, is recalled by this sketch of the '77 Gate and, in the background, the Widener Memorial Library at Harvard.

A member of the class of '07, Harry Elkins Widener, at the age of 26, had a library of 3000 volumes and the respect of book-collectors throughout America and Europe. It was in 1912, after he had attended the Huth sale in London, that he uttered his fateful words. Tucking a rare second Edition of Bacon's essays in his pocket, he turned to a friend and remarked, "I think I'll take this little Bacon with me and if I am shipwrecked it will go down with me."

A few days later he perished when the Titanic went down in mid-Atlantic.

A LOOK AT EARLY BOSTON

FRANKLIN place (now Franklin street) Boston, looked like this before the once residential district was changed to a business section, and the name changed to Franklin Street. Originally marsh and bog land, the section below what is now Hawley street was unimproved until Joseph Barrell, Esq., a merchant who lived on Summer street, laid it out for a pleasure garden. In 1793 two rows of brick houses were erected on the spot, and a small plot fenced and ornamented with a monumental urn commemorative of Benjamin Franklin.

The urn was obtained in Bath, England, by Bulfinch. The sketch shows the section, looking toward Arch street, as it appeared before the warehouses were built. The urn was moved to Mt. Auburn cemetery, and now stands upon the lot on Bellwort path, leading from Walnut avenue.

THE FIRST DEPARTMENT STORE IN THE UNITED STATES

THE bleak looking building in this sketch is a faithful replica of what is regarded by historians as the first trading post in New England, and probably in the United States. It served the Indians, the Pilgrims and the Dutch who sailed over from New York. The original "department store" was built in 1627 by the Plymouth Mayflower colonists and was known as the Aptucxet Trading Post. The present structure was officially opened Sept. 3, 1930.

The land was provided by the Bourne Historical Society and the General Society of Mayflower Descendants raised the money. It is situated in Bourne village on the banks of the Cape Cod canal in Massachusetts. The plans were drawn by the architect, Joseph Everett Chandler.

THE BUILDING WHICH MAKES A FACE

IN fact, the Harvard Lampoon building, Cambridge, Mass., makes many faces, if one is in imaginative mood and views it in several lights. And many faces have been made at it, because of its always amusingly erratic editorial antics of the past. Verily, the sacred Ibis has never had a more unusual perch. Edmund Wheelwright, an architect who specialized in the unusual, apparently was in harmony with that melange of editorial individualities which is the Lampoon publishing policy when he designed the structure.

Seen from the front, in the light of the setting sun, one may imagine the facade to be a gigantic and Rabelaisian face. The lurid windows seem to be eyes, the extended lamp a predatory beak and the doorway a mouth. The ibis on the roof might be taken for a wisp of hair, upcurled, perhaps, as if in astonishment at the copy ground out below.

THE "THEN & NOW" HOUSE

THE attractive home shown in the sketch is at 35 Beacon street, Boston, and exemplifies the changes in ideas and other factors of the times. It was built shortly after the War of 1812 and is a splendid example of the architecture of the era. Dignified and serene, it snuggles beside its towering neighbor, "The Tudor"

In those days of the 1800's there were but two large rooms and one small one on each floor in the grand manner of the times. But today, each floor contains seven rooms and three baths.

However, the present rooms are not crowded. The whole is a remarkably effective and coherent result, in keeping and harmony with the rest of the building. This renovation was done under the supervision of one of Beacon Hill's best contemporary architects, who kept the feeling and simplicity typical of the house itself.

JACK FROST
1935

COPY OF AN ELIZABETHAN HOUSE, THE OCCUPANTS OF WHICH WITHSTOOD THE BLACK PLAGUE

AT 19 Commonwealth avenue, near Lake street, Newton, Mass., is the home pictured, which is an authentic copy of the Providence House of Chester, England, the occupants of which escaped infection during the Black Plague. Both houses bear the inscription "God's Providence is Mine Inheritance". The original house was built in 1632, and the American copy was completed in 1903. It has one of the finest gardens in metropolitan Boston and a splendid view of the reservoir.

A PIG CAUSED THE FORMATION OF OUR SENATE AND HOUSE OF REPRESENTATIVES

WHEN one looks at the Massachusetts State House he thinks only of the architectural beauty of what is one of the oldest capitols in the country. The gleaming dome and red-brick major portion of the building hold the attention of passers-by. The onlooker would hardly believe that the Senate and House were really formed through the involuntary co-operation of a pig.

However, they did have their beginnings in the controversy begun originally in a trifling law suit during the Colonial rule of Governor Winthrop who tells the story:

He says, "There fell out a great business upon a very small occasion. Anno 1636 there was a stray sow in Boston, which was brought to Captain Keayne; he had

it cried divers times, and divers came to see it, but none made claim to it for near a year. He kept it in his yard with a sow of his own. Afterwards, one Sherman's wife, having lost such a sow, laid claim to it," and thus the discourse runs a few pages.

This affair, during which Mrs. Sherman sued Keayne and lost money to him and kept referring the case to court for numerous years, finally resulted in a great dispute between the magistrates and deputies as concerned the "negative voice." This led to the final separation by written resolution, of the Legislature of Massachusetts into two separate and co-ordinate branches — deputies and magistrates, which we now term representatives and senators. This separation was listed in the Colonial Records of March 7, 1644, and was a notable step toward constitutional government.

OLD CHURCH NAMES BOSTON SQUARE

THE New South Church at Church Green, Bedford and Summer streets, Boston, prior to 1872. This structure was built about 1728 and was razed just prior to the fire of 1872, according to the records of the Bostonian Society (a strange coincidence of numbers incidentally).

On the left is Bedford street and at the right, Summer street, looking in the direction of Washington street. The square in the center is still listed in the city directory as Church Green, although office buildings now occupy the site of the church.

On the immediate right are several large private residences with the fancy iron grille work fences so popular in that day. The home of Daniel Webster was located not far from this vicinity.

MACY'S FRONT DOOR IN NANTUCKET

THE fan-shaped doorway of the old Macy house at Nantucket is generally acclaimed as the most beautiful on the island. It has been widely copied by architects for use in all parts of the country. In the house have lived a long line of distinguished sons of Nantucket, including Gen. George Nelson Macy, provost-general in the civil war, Edwin Macy Stanton, secretary of war under President Lincoln, and Rowland H. Macy, who gave up the sea for a trader's life and founded Macy's store in New York in 1858. The house was built in 1790.

WHAT OLIVER WENDELL HOLMES EXPECTED IN THE NEXT WORLD

NOT trumpeting angels, nor pearly gates, but the vista of Tufts College in Medford, Mass., as it looked during his lifetime and as it looks in the sketch, was what Oliver Wendell Holmes expected to see first when he opened his eyes in the world beyond death. That, at least, is what the great American physician and author told William Dean Howells before he passed away in 1894.

The sketch shows Tufts in the Holmes era, viewed from Powder House square, Medford. From right to left atop the hill are: East hall, Middle hall, West hall (in the rear), Ballou hall and two homes of instructors in Professors row. The road near the foreground is College avenue.

JACK FROST
1936

AMERICA'S OLDEST CLUBHOUSE

THE Country Club, at 191 Clyde street, Brookline, Mass., is recognized as the oldest country club in the United States, in point of continued existence. The idea of the club was first proposed May 29, 1860, dropped then because of the civil war, and renewed later with the actual founding taking place in April, 1882, at the home of J. Murray Forbes, 107 Commonwealth avenue. Occupying the site of the old Clyde park and adjoining lands acquired during the years, the club covers 226 acres, part of which at one time belonged to Daniel Webster. Its golf course was the scene of the U. S. amateur championships in 1910, 1922 and 1934, and the U. S. open was played there in 1913. A. Windsor Weld is now president, and the club has 901 regular, 106 associate, three honorary and two army and navy members.

In its early days The Country Club was primarily a horse club. Shortly after its opening, the club absorbed the Myopia Club of Winchester, which was founded in 1879.

JOHN MARTIN'S HOUSE NOW OWNED BY COLONIAL DAMES OF AMERICA

THE John Martin House, on Route 20 in Swansea, near Providence, R. I., was built in 1728. At the rear is a "bolling green" with well sweeps, and inside the house are pieces of historic interest.

The house, now the property of the Massachusetts Society of Colonial Dames of America, will be open to the public from June 1 to Nov. 1. A direct descendant of the builder of the house bequeathed it to the society.

Old records show that John Martin bought the property from John Devotion and Richard Haile Sept. 23, 1715, and the deed was recorded in Taunton, Sept. 28, 1724. In 1728 Martin moved to Swansea from Rehoboth and built the house on the site he had purchased. He lived in it until his death.

A MAN WHO SITS UP IN HIS GRAVE

ONE R. J. Smith of Amesbury, Mass., was so fond of sitting in his easy chair during the last, mellow years of his life that he resented the possibility of death separating him from such comfort. So, according to legend, he provided in his will for burial in a sitting position in a marble tomb in Amesbury's Mount Prospect cemetery. His request was carried out in the late '90's.

The marble tomb disintegrated some time ago, but a structure of field stone has been erected over the grave and, so far as any one knows, the chair is intact. Three white birches shadow the site in summer.

ROOF OF THIS HOUSE TOUCHES THE GROUND

THE artist has hunted constantly for a house whose roof touches the ground, and the answer is the quaint historic Jackson House at Portsmouth, N. H. As can be seen in the sketch, the roof touches the snow, and in the summer, the edge of the roof is only a few inches from the earth.

The old timer has much the same flavor as the House of the Seven Gables in Salem, and is the oldest home in Portsmouth. It was built in 1664 by Robert Jackson, and is situated on Northwest street. The frame of the house is of oak, and the timbers for the sills project into the lower rooms. The sloping roof is its dominant feature.

JACK FROST
1935

GOVERNOR SHIRLEY'S SEASIDE MANSION NOW IN ROXBURY

IN the days of his colonial governorship, it was the custom of William Shirley to walk from his home to his private landing, where his shallop was moored. He would then sail two miles and a half to Windmill point, which was about where the South Station now stands, and would travel in the Governor's carriage to the State House.

The house has been moved only 30 feet, but the filling in of the land has carried the seashore some distance away, whereas formerly it was only a short distance down Shirley street. The house was built after 1746, is known as the Shirley-Eustis house, and is rapidly going to pieces.

Jack Frost

RESIDENTIAL STREET OF STABLES

THE quaint little street which runs from 10 River street to 70 Brimmer, Boston, is shown in the sketch as it looked in the late afternoon when the long shadows began to be absorbed by the growing dusk. Strangely, Byron street was all stables on the left side and all houses on the Beacon street side when it was laid out in 1830.

The homes of the many residents of this short street once served as shelter to the carriages and horses of the Beacon Hillers of a more old fashioned day. The Hotel Lincolnshire can be seen in the background. This street was formerly called B street.

MARK TWAIN'S HOME NOW A MEMORIAL LIBRARY

IT is indeed fitting that the home of one of America's foremost and most beloved authors of homely stories should be used today as a library and museum. The rambling structure pictured was built by Mark Twain whose real name was Samuel Langhorne Clemens in 1873. He lived here till 1891, the period during which many of his most famous novels were published. "A Tramp Abroad", "The Gilded Age", conjointly with C. D. Warner "Adventures of Tom Sawyer", "Adventures of Huckleberry Finn", "A Yankee at the Court of King Arthur", were among these.

Now this house serves both as the Hartford Public Library and as a Museum. This memorial to Mark Twain, who certainly ranks with Hawthorne as a master of style and human interest in the American novel, is well worth visiting. There is a most unusual design running between the lower windows, for all the world like that of an Indian blanket. The house, atop a hill, is at 351 Farmington avenue, Hartford, Connecticut.

JACK FROST

MARBLEHEAD POWDER HOUSE SERVED USE IN THREE WARS

MARBLEHEAD, Massachusetts is filled with places of historic and human interest. Weeks could be spent in browsing and study there, even if it is of small population and slight geographic proportions. The quaint Agnes Surriage Well; Ye Old Brig, birthplace of Molly Pitcher; The Old Spite House with its side yard picket fence; the reproduction of the 10th century castle of Leif the Lucky's parents, called the "Brahtalid"; and myriad other points worthy of a visit abound in this seapost town, unspoiled by the stream of summer pilgrims.

As picturesque as any other landmark there, and most important among relics of historic import, is The Powder House. It is a small, circular, brick magazine, situated on what is now known as Green street, but what was formerly called "The Ferry Road". It was built by vote of the town at the outbreak of the "French and Indian War", and not only served as a cache for ammunition at that time, but was utilized during both the Revolution and the War of 1812.

As companion in spirit to this little shrine, is one of Whittier's most famous subjects. Although only the site remains, the bridge which inspired John Greenleaf Whittier's "The Wishing Bridge" was also situated on the old Ferry Road. It spanned a small stream that ran through Steer Swamp, and was not, as so many think today, near the Devereux Mansion.

BOSTON'S ONLY FLYING BUTTRESS A FAKE

FLYING buttresses are as thick as flies in Rheims, Cologne and Bourges, and as thick as zabaglioni in Florence, but they seem rare in Boston. In fact, Monsieur, Herr, Signor Fancy This finds but one, and that serves not to support the Church of the Covenant at Newbury and Berkeley streets in Boston, but merely acts as an ornament. Buttresses usually fly in pairs — that is, there is one on the opposite side of a structure to offset the push of the other side—and when there is but one, it may be termed a mere architectural fantasy or fake. No one, however, would begrudge the Church of the Covenant its extraneous buttress, for it adds definitely to the attractiveness of the pile.

TREE GROWS AROUND A GRAVESTONE

IN a friendly, fir-fringed mountain cemetery nestled in the town of Tamworth, New Hampshire, stands a freak of nature which has riveted the attention of many a stroller. It is a tree which "came between a father and his daughter". It was probably self-sown, and is probably the only tree in this cemetery. It grew between the head stones of one Perkins Moulton and his daughter, buried side by side within a year of each other, and has enveloped at least a third of the girl's slate stone and pushed it several inches further beneath the ground. The stones are decorated with the usual weeping willow design, and Mr. Moulton's bears the date of May 24, 1852, his death.

One can't be absolutely sure that it is the daughter and not the mother beside Perkins Moulton, for the tree covers part of the lateral surface, while lichen and moss pretty thoroughly encrust the rest. The name Betty is discernible, and because the name Perkins on the stone at the right is followed by the "&" sign so that the wife's (the mother's) name is probably hidden beneath the tree, it seems reasonably safe to assume that this is the daughter.

"EXPELLED" FROM FOUR TOWNS, BUT LATER MARRIED AARON BURR

THE most romantic story associated with Rutland, Massachusetts, now noted for its fine State Sanatorium and Cottage Sanatoria for the treatment of tuberculosis, is that of Betsey Bowen, better known as Madam Jumel. She, her sister Polly, mother Phoebe and step-father Jonathan Clark lived for nearly three years in a "Dug-Out" about where the gate of "Goose Hill" Cemetery, New Boston, now stands. This gateway, pictured, is veritably surrounded by an air of fascination when one learns of the unbelievable career of this girl who, with her whole family, was expelled from Providence, later from Rehoboth, Taunton, North Brookfield, and when they left Rutland went to North Carolina.

Her father was a sailor who was lost at sea about 1780. Ten years after that her mother remarried.

About 1806 Betsey married Stephen Jumel, a rich San Dominican merchant who made a fortune in West India goods, and was a noted sportsman. She lived with him in Paris in regal splendor for many years, and fraternized with nobility and even royalty. She educated herself so that she became an accomplished writer and patron of music and art. Later, less wealthy, they came to New York where she began to repair her husband's fortune. "She used to ride to Saratoga and Balston in a chariot drawn by eight horses—". Jumel died in 1832. Then Madam Jumel married Aaron Burr, ex-Vice-President of the United States, but was divorced in about a year.

ARCHITECTURAL CHANGE CAUSED BY SOIL

ORIGINAL plans for the building of Holy Cross Cathedral in Boston, (like those for the spireless towers of Notre Dame in Paris) included two crowning steeples. The architects believed the whole structure would be more harmonious and pleasing to the eye with these spires, but the shakiness of the subsoil forced them to compromise. The towers one sees today are not of the intended shapes.

So Mother Earth, which theoretically gave a leaning to the Tower of Pisa, had something to do with the making of a cathedral of the mother church. Of interest to some of the millions who have viewed the cathedral is the fact that the tower on the left encases what seems to be either a ship's mast or a flagpole.

HISTORIC HOUSE IN MAINE —THAT TUTT BUILT"

THE Ruggles House in Columbia Falls, Maine, which was constructed after a design by Aaron Sherman of Duxbury, Massachusetts, was built about 1820 for Judge Thomas Ruggles, a wealthy lumber dealer. The house is noted for its delicately detailed exterior trim and expertly beautiful carvings throughout. Arthur Train, the brilliant writer of contemporary fame, used the Ruggles house as the setting for his short story, "The House that Tutt Built".

Most villagers state that the populace of the town was once so impressed by the unearthly beauty of the swastika design below the mantel of the dining room that they believed the carver's knife was guided by the hand of an angel. The present connotation of the swastika has undoubtedly dispelled that illusion! Columbia Falls is very proud of this landmark and it is now in the process of restoration.

THE CHURCH OF THE ADVENT

THE Church of the Advent, on quiet Brimmer street, is a Boston monument to a great religious movement which originated in England in the nineteenth century—the Oxford movement.

The present Church, a mecca for hundreds of Bostonians who prefer the ritualistic, or "high church," Episcopal service, is the fourth place of worship for the Parish of the Advent since William Croswell and a little band of laymen organized on Advent Sunday, 1844. A church was built on Green street in 1847, and the congregation moved to Bowdoin street in 1864.

The Brimmer street building was first used on Easter Day, 1879, when the Rev. Charles C. Grafton was rector. The architect was John H. Sturgis, a communicant of the parish. The dignified and beautiful building is admirably contrived to make the best use of an awkward piece of land.

JACK FROST
L.N.B. MD.
Winthrop Place

"FIRST ROUGH GRANITE HOME—"

THE house pictured above was the first rough granite home in which the stone was used with no hammering of the face. It was built by Samuel Cabot on Winthrop place, Boston, and occupied from 1823 to 1833. In the rear was "Thorndike's Pasture", many feet below the street level.

The structure, really two houses, had a 64-foot front and a roof of matched boards and best Welch slate, with of course the customary wine closet and milk cellar. There was also a large garden or yard on Winthrop Place, with a grass plot in the center and trees on the side. Boston's contemporary Samuel Cabot lives at Jamaica Plain near the Jamaica Pond.

Dochet Island
JACK FROST, 1938

"MAINE ISLAND WHICH 'CHASES THE TOURIST'"

THE long, flat island above, surmounted by buildings and a lighthouse is very famous in the eastern part of Maine, both as an historical spot and as an oddity. The odd angle is that for many, many, times its own length, this bit of land seems to remain opposite the traveling automobile. This illusion is probably accounted for by the way the road beside the St. Croix river, in which it is situated, winds around.

The historical associations of this island, called Dochet Island and reached by rowboat from Red Beach, are with Pierre du Guast, the Sieur de Monts and his lieutenant, Samuel de Champlain. They, with fourscore colonists among which there was a Catholic priest and a Huguenot minister, landed here in June 26, 1604. de Monts called it St. Croix, and expected to establish there a trading post and settlement. A severe winter and scurvy wrought such discouragement that in 1605 they left the island, using it only as a French garrison.

This chance settlement of this island determined the adjustment of the boundary question at the end of the Revolutionary War. Both the United States and Great Britain acknowledged the River St. Croix as the point of departure in drawing the line, but England disputed the American claim on what river bore this name. The discovery of Champlain's map and the ensuing examination of the ruins of the island settlement decided the matter. Had the British won their point, this part of eastern Maine would doubtless now be Canadian territory.

THE STORY BEHIND THE FIRST CHURCH IN ROXBURY

THE history of the First Church in Roxbury, Mass., is bound up with the story of John Eliot, one of its founders, best known as the Apostle to the Indians. The church, shown in the above sketch, stands in Eliot square, Roxbury, and is one of Boston's many historic shrines visited each year by thousands of tourists. Its architecture is dignified and it contains many historical treasures.

Eliot, who, translated both the Old and New Testaments into the Indian language and labored for years as a missionary among the aborigines, had much to do with the organization of the First Church parish, which was founded in 1630-31.

Although he is popularly believed to have been the first minister of the church, he was actually an auxiliary minister, never assuming official charge of the parish. He was the most famous in a long line of distinguished men who have been identified with the ancient church organization.

HOUSES BUILT AROUND THE CORNER FROM THEIR FRONT ENTRANCES

ON Beacon Hill, Boston, which holds many memories of early Boston, may be found the two quaintest houses in the city. These dwellings, built at the end of Sentry Hill Place, are part of an odd device for closing a street when the land falls abruptly to a lower level. What looks like a two-story double house at the end of Sentry Hill place is in reality a false front. Passing through either of the doors the visitor finds himself in a narrow hallway, with a brick wall at the rear built up from Primus avenue 50 feet below.

From either side of this hallway steps lead up into narrow houses actually built on the two sides of Sentry Hill place. Each floor of the upper two stories of these dwellings has only two rooms. The lower part of each merges into walls built up from Primus avenue. The houses are thus built "Around the Corner" from their front entrances.

JACK FROST
1935

HOUSE WITH FRONT ENTRANCE AT REAR

AT 7 Buckingham place, Cambridge, is the house shown in the sketch. The doorway pictured faces the street, and is the rear entrance, at the back of the house. The front door is where the back should be, facing an inner garden. The reason for this rests with the builder of this house, and two others on the same street, treated in the same manner. The present occupants of the house, Dr. and Mrs. Henry J. Cadbury, are very much satisfied with this unconventional plan, and believe that in that fact, and the wooden floor of the cellar, rests the attraction which the building has for them.

HISTORIC RHODE ISLAND HOUSE IN A GRAVEYARD

THE residence of Mr. Austen G. Fox in Wickford, Rhode Island, is of considerable historic interest. It is an old mansion on the estate of the Cocumcussoc Farm, and originally called the Smith Block House.

It literally rests in a cemetery, for in the yard in front of the house a bronze tablet marks the grave of forty colonists who died in the Great Swamp Fight in the King Philip's Wars. The records indicate that this house was built in 1638, burned by the Indians in 1675 and re-built in 1678 in its present form. A huge, ancient fireplace with several clever mechanical contrivances serves to add interest to the low-roofed interior.

The building was also known in earlier times as the Roger Williams Trading Post. In fact, it was undoubtedly the home of Roger Williams for a number of years, thereby associating itself more deeply with the history of the state of Rhode Island.

TYPICALLY "SHAKER"

THE stone platform with its graceful iron railing is found at "Fruitlands & The Wayside Museums, Inc.", the land of Lost Utopias atop Prospect Hill at Harvard, Massachusetts. Miss Clara Endicott Sears has gathered hereon valuable relics of the three famous quests for happiness, Alcott's Fruitlands, American Indian Museum, and Old Shaker House. Mother Ann Lee was the founder of the Shakers, the name derived from Society of Shaking Quakers as they were first called. Among other places where the Shakers settled are Livingston County, N.Y., Enfield, Connecticut, and Watervliet near Troy, N.Y., all of which, except for a small settlement at Hancock, Mass., have gone.

The *"alighting platform"* above was used by the *Shaker sisters when descending from their horses or carriages,* it being one of the precepts of their Society to avoid anything that would necessitate physical contact with the opposite sex.

"20 LOUISBURG SQUARE"

JENNY LIND, the "Swedish Nightingale," was married to her accompanist, Otto Goldschmidt on Feb. 5, 1852, in this Beacon Hill home, which was then the residence of S. G. Ward. For a long period the singer was feted by Boston society.

Her appearance in this country was brought about through P. T. Barnum in 1850. Her first Boston recital was given in Tremont Temple, Sept. 11, 1850, and was attended by the elite of Boston. At one of her concerts it was reported at the time, Ossian Euclid Dodge, a vocalist and composer, paid a premium of $625 for tickets.

THE STORY BEHIND THE MAN WHO "WAS JOHN HARVARD"

AN interesting, but little known fact, is that the famous Daniel French statue of John Harvard which is in the Harvard Yard is an ideal likeness. The sculptor, was commissioned to do a statute of John Harvard, who left half of his estate and 260 books to aid in constructing the college which became Harvard. Being unable to find a picture of John Harvard, the sculptor decided to do a likeness of "a typical Harvard student." What few people also know is that the person selected for this honor was Mr. Sherman Hoar. And much, as if this signal piece of fortune should have marked him for things good, Sherman Hoar's star reached considerable height.

He was born in Concord, Massachusetts, July 30, 1860 and died there on October 7, 1898 in the same room in which he was born.

He was graduated from the Phillips Exeter Academy in 1878, from Harvard College in 1882, and from Harvard Law School in 1885. Hoar practiced law in Waltham, Mass., for two years, then in Boston for three years as partner of the late Moorfield Storey. Later he was elected to Congress as a Democrat and served one term. He managed Cleveland's 1892 campaign in Massachusetts, and served as U. S. District Attorney 1893-1897. The statute itself was given to the University in 1884 by Samuel James Bridge (s) who attained the honorary degree of master of arts in 1880.

"SHAKESPEAREAN" TOWER ATOP A MASSACHUSETTS CHURCH

THE quaint little edifice shown in the sketch is that of the North Parish of North Andover, Mass., Unitarian, and founded in 1645. The present church is about a century old, and is modeled after another which was on the same spot. A Paul Revere Bell hangs in the tower, and a most fascinating chronology of the Parish and activities rests below the pulpit in the form of an old minister's book dating from 1810. The latter was begun by the Reverend Bailey Loring and ends with the final entries of minister emeritus, the Reverend Samuel C. Beane. The present head of the parish, Reverend Cornelis Heyn, has written a very interesting permanent sermon inspired by this 128 year record.

Travelers from this section of Massachusetts have stopped in astonishment at the spectacle of the attractively situated Holy Trinity Church of Stratford-upon-Avon; for nostalgia inspired, at first unaccountably, by this structure reflected so peacefully in the nearby river, makes them think immediately of home. The reason, is the remarkable resemblance of their Unitarian Church in North Andover to this landmark of the country of William Shakespeare. The steeple is almost a reproduction, while the feeling of the entire tower is vaguely like this English building. Clock placed differently, and three instead of two gothic windows on the facade are the main contrasts.

A MAN WHO HAS BEEN ENTERING HIS OWN TOMB FOR FIFTY-EIGHT YEARS

THE life-like statute above is that of John P. Bowman, who, till his death in 1891, lived in a large home opposite the present location of Laurel Glen Cemetery at Cuttingsville, Vermont. This home is kept in readiness at all times anticipating the return of Mr. Bowman, his wife, Jennie, and their two daughters, who preceded him in death. Inside the Mausoleum are a bust of himself, and of his wife who died in 1880, a life-sized statue of his daughter, Addie L. Bowman; also large mirrors, several chairs, a huge granite door, mosaic floor and three caskets. The residence nearby is always lighted in the evening, and details such as grass and shrubbery are attended.

Mr. Bowman has the key to the tomb and his hat in one hand and carries a wreath in the other. Inside is the inscription: "A couch of dreamless sleep. To the memory of a sainted wife and daughters." The other daughter, not represented by sculpture, was Ella H. Bowman, who was born in 1856 and died in 1879. Hundreds of Vermont tourists go out of their way each summer to visit this unique shrine.

THE ONLY ROLLING DAM IN THE COUNTRY

AN industrial center of the early Newton colony in Massachusetts was at Bemis. Here David Bemis built a mill that turned out the first sail-cloth in this country. Later the New England cotton sails carried ships of all nations through the seven seas.

Bemis, where the Charles River still tumbles, has supposedly the only "Rolling Dam" in the country, built in 1778. The flood of several springs ago threatened the dam, but it held.

Bemis' mill was also reputedly the first building in the United States to be illuminated by gas, an enterprising innovation in days when mill hands worked fourteen hours a day.

JACK FROST
1935

"THE ONLY RESPECTABLE STREET IN AMERICA"

ALTHOUGH Henry James, more an Englishman in spirit than he was an American, was infinitely more familiar with the Strand and Mayfair in London than he was with the public ways of American cities, he yet felt expert enough to pronounce Mt. Vernon street, Boston, the only respectable one in America.

That the street still is respectable is an indubitable truth, however one may disagree with the scope of the great novelist's comparison. When Arnold Bennett inspected Boston, he dashed some local prides by refusing to call the city "quite English." He would go no further than to say that perhaps Boston was the least un-English of American cities. Certainly Mt. Vernon street has a less un-English look than many streets, and that may have been why James liked it.

ONE OF BUT TWO INSTANCES OF HOUSES WITHOUT LAND WHATEVER ATTACHED

THE Gleaner Papers or some similar book mentions that in 1885, the lofts over the arch on India Wharf, Boston, and the apartments over the arch in Franklin Place, were the only two instances of fee simple estates without any land whatever attached to them. The former bit of architecture belonged to John Lowell, Jr., and the latter was conveyed by Charles Vaughan, William Scollay and Charles Bulfinch to the Massachusetts Historical Society in consideration of five shillings on May 1, 1794. This transfer of "the upper apartment or room in the centre building in Franklin Place in Boston, called the Crescent, with the passageway or staircase leading to the same" was for the promotion of the designs of this Society.

The equally famous Bostonian Society furnished the material for the above sketch which shows a view of the section of town where the above-mentioned apartments were to be found. The familiar curve of the present-day Franklin street is about the only thing that resembles that downtown thoroughfare as it is above depicted as it appeared just prior to the great Boston fire of 1872.

The picture shows the cathedral building, the few remaining trees at that time and what was known as the Bulfinch crescent development.

JACK FROST
1935

ELITE STREET BUILT OVER HOOPS FROM SKIRTS

THAT the patrician houses of Commonwealth avenue and other streets in the Back Bay section of Boston stand on what was a city dump is a fact, but that the dump was largely filled with cast-off hoops from the skirts of Victorian ladies is a Boston legend possibly founded on fact. Certain it is that while the swampy district was being filled in, the last hoop skirt was laid at rest. Some of the wearers were sentimental enough to embalm the skirts in closets, but others, with the impetuousness of ladies turning to new styles, may indeed have had them trundled away by the ashman.

Pictured are two houses which look as though their foundations are solid enough, be they made of hoop-skirts or ashes. They are at 2 and 4 Commonwealth avenue. No. 2 is the Boston Engineers club.

WHAT ABOUT THE HORSE WITHOUT A TONGUE?

THE British, it is said, can't see a joke. But they are observant, nonetheless, as seen by the fact that it took English Author S. P. B. Mais (who wrote "A Modern Columbus"), to discover that Sculptor Thomas Ball failed to equip the spirited charger in the Washington equestrian monument in the Boston Public Garden with a tongue. The original model of the "tongueless horse" statue is now preserved in the Boston Athenaeum.

That is one story. There is, however, a strong argument, supported by one of our greatest living sculptors, maintaining that this famous horse HAS a tongue. This sculptor states that the tongue is pressed against the roof of the mouth in such a way that it cannot be seen from the ground.

When the story of this supposed error first became circulated, it swept the entire country, gathering impetus as it travelled. It became almost a national myth, with the added "angle" that when the sculptor realized he had forgotten the horse's tongue, he committed suicide. The fact that the creator was active at his home in Montclair, N. H., even at the age of 91 would seem to belie this added point.

SITE OF THE FIRST CRUSADES AGAINST "RUM"

HOUSES in Rockport, Mass., still standing where in 1856 women hatchet gangs met to plan a raid on "demon rum shops." The women who took part in the raid were all arrested and found guilty in lower court of breaking and entering but were freed of the charge by the state supreme court in 1859.

A TOUCH OF HOLLAND IN EASTHAM, MASS.

DIAGONALLY across the highway from the town hall of Eastham is this quaint windmill. It is the oldest windmill now on Cape Cod, according to the townspeople.

One result of the Pilgrim's stay in Holland is the interesting and artistic windmills which are on the Cape today. This one is on the main route to Provincetown, and was rebuilt a short time ago by the town of Eastham. An old miller was employed to grind the grain of the tourist or citizen who was interested — and thousands were. The old vanes turned in the sunlight, and under the guidance of John Fulcher, miller, flour was turned out in the manner of the early settlers.

FROM SYNAGOGUE TO CHURCH TO CABARET

ON Warrenton street behind the Hotel Bradford in Boston, is this picturesque building which has undergone several unusual transformations. It was built in 1843, and was the home of the first Jewish congregation in Boston. Later it was purchased by a Scotch Presbyterian congregation, and served as a church. For the past 12 years it has been a cabaret. The building has beautiful lines, partly concealed by the signs over its front.

THE HOUSE THROUGH WHICH AUTOMOBILES PASS

SHOWN in the sketch is the entrance to Charles River Square which lies to the right of the foot of Revere street, looking toward the Charles River Basin, Boston. The homes are all facing an attractive center, and although there is a main entrance on Embankment road, this curved tunnel, facing on Revere Street is much used.

It goes through No. 16 Charles River Square, and owes its origin to Frank Bourne, architect, who arranged for its construction when planning the details of the square. The accommodating house has sacrificed much space for the passageway, but the entrance, with its quiet sign is picturesque, although modern.

VARIEGATED WAGON-WHEEL FENCE OF FRIENDSHIP

DOVER boasts of one of the most original of hobbies. A highly decorative wagon-wheel fence borders the drive of Miss Amelia Peabody at her Dover, Mass., residence, "Mill Farm." Wagon wheels are her passion, it seems, and each painted wheel on the fence represents a friend. At one time some one endeavored to sell her a wheel—but in vain. For she thought it would mean nothing, being purchased from a stranger.

The wheels have been up about two years, although Miss Peabody has been collecting these sentimental cartwheels over a period of years.

THE CHURCH BUILT OVER FOUR HUNDRED GRAVES

FEW people know that the remains of 400 persons remain under King's Chapel today. The church is really over the cemetery. When the Church of England wanted land to build a church in this country, no one was willing to sell any land, so Gov. Andros appropriated a portion of the burying ground.

Because of awkward methods of quarrying the granite, the original church was five years building, and when it was completed, King's Chapel, located on Tremont street, Boston, was the first granite structure ever built in this country. The cemetery beneath it was started in 1630, and the church was completed in 1689. The cornerstone of the present building was laid Aug. 11, 1749, by Gov. William Shirley.

Jack Frost

CHRISTIAN SCIENCE PRESERVATION OF BEAUTY

IT is seldom in this modern age that convenience is sacrificed to beauty, but when the publishing house was built near the Christian Science Church, Mother Church in Boston, shown above, it was constructed low and wide to preserve the view of the church dome from as many angles as possible. Moreover, the church was given a grassy frontage, free of buildings, facing Huntington avenue to give it a proper setting. Charles Brigham was the architect who designed the church.

A GLIMPSE OF OLD BOSTON

A TYPICAL scene of Tremont street, Boston, at the north side of Boylston street in the 1850's. In the background is the Winthrop house, long since torn down, which was on the present site of Masonic Temple. In the foreground at the right is one of the open cars of the Metropolitan Horse railroad. The open car service was discontinued in the 1860's. Tremont street was a busy thoroughfare for those days.

This sketch was made from a photograph taken about 1856 and which is now on file at the rooms of the Bostonian Society, Old State House.

AMERICA'S ONLY IRISH ROUND TOWER

STANDING in St. Mary's cemetery in Milford, Mass., is this striking tower. It is a replica of the famous round towers of Ireland. After diligent search, David Davidson and Clinton L. Barnard failed to find or hear of another one in America.

It was built about 1895 by a great lover of Ireland and Irish history, the late Rev. Patrick Cuddihy. He was for many years the pastor of St. Mary's Roman Catholic Church in Milford and an authentic source of facts relating to Irish history.

JACK FROST
1935

A 258 YEAR OLD HOUSE IN A MODERN SCHOOLYARD

ON Harvard street, Brookline, Mass., is the Edward Devotion school. Its two brick components are on either side of the house pictured, this giving the effect of the house being in the midst of a schoolyard.

The man after whom the school was named, lived in the house some time. It was built in 1680 by his father or grandfather. When he died, Edward Devotion left 739 pounds 4 shillings for the erection of a school, but it met with other usage. His grandfather, also Edward, was one of the first settlers of Muddy River—or Brookline.

ENCLOSURE WITH CANNON FOR FENCE POSTS

FORT WASHINGTON, a spot so little known that even information booths at subway stations don't know about it, is located beside a soap factory at the foot of Albany street, near Waverly, in the vicinity of Central square, Cambridge, Mass. The fort was built under Washington during the siege of Boston and is attractive because of its simplicity.

A fine fence surrounds the plot, part of which is shown (to the left of the entrance), with posts in the shape of cannon and the ball atop the muzzle. The cannons are similar to the 30-pounder inside the fort and show an instructive originality on the part of those who constructed the fence.

This type of fence is extremely rare. The pickets represent battle axes and javelin-like spears.

HIDDEN TREASURE AMONG THE STONES OF WIDENER MEMORIAL LIBRARY

HARVARD'S Widener Library is one of the foremost libraries of its kind in the world. It was erected in memory of her son, Harry Elkins Widener, by Mrs. George D. Widener of Philadelphia. She laid its cornerstone in 1913.

The secret of the hidden treasure is that cornerstone. For among the objects placed inside was a collection of all coins, including gold pieces, in use in the United States at that time.

The library cost approximately $2,000,000. As it stands facing the yard, with its corinthian colonade above the columns and pilasters 40 feet from the ground, one thinks for a moment that the young collector who met a tragic fate, has a contrastingly beautiful and appropriate memorial. He was a member of the class of 1907.

ANCIENT BEACON STREET HOUSE IS ON WALNUT STREET

THE home of the Judge Baker Guidance Center is shown in the sketch. Although it is one of the best looking houses numbered on Beacon street, Boston, it is one of the oldest, since it was the first brick house erected on that street.

Although it bears the number 38½ Beacon street, it is really on Walnut street, according to present-day classification, as its front entrance faces on Walnut. It was built in 1804 by John Phillips, first mayor of Boston. His distinguished son, Wendell Phillips, was born here Nov. 29, 1811.

Lt.-Gov. Thomas Lindall Winthrop, Thomas Dixon, counsel for the Netherlands, and Nathan Matthews, who gave Matthews Hall to Harvard, were among the noted persons who made their home here.

JACK FROST

FAMOUS HOUSE LEASED FOR 1000 YEARS AT A PENNY A YEAR

THE Apthorp House, known to the world, but almost hidden from Cambridge, has been the subject of much discussion in its history. About 1802 one Timothy Lindall Jennison, physician, leased the easterly half of this historic house to Thomas Warland for 10 centuries "at the rent of one cent per year—if the house shall so long stand and endure." These two also paid only $1 for the title to the house held by Jonathan Simp-

son, senior warden of Christ Church.

This dormitory of Harvard, once General Israel Putnam's headquarters and Burgoyne's prison, was built for his wife by the Rev. East Apthorp, first rector of the new Christ Church, and is between Plympton and Linden streets, Cambridge. The third story of the building, according to one tradition, was added to provide room for the slaves of John Borland.

PAUL REVERE TOOK A DARE

PAUL REVERE was one of the most versatile men in the history of New England. A silversmith, artist, engraver, patriot, soldier, his other enterprises went as far as making false teeth and bell-casting. It is this latter angle which interests us this time.

For there was not a man in the Commonwealth who would dare to take the commission for a bell in King's chapel. It was stipulated that the caster would have to turn out a bell of the same weight, size, and TONE as the original which was to be recast. However, this did not daunt Revere; he took the risk and the result was a bell which fitted the specifications—except that the tone of his bell was sweeter than the other.

Revere's home in North square, off North street, Boston, a shrine for tourists, is shown in the sketch, nestling between the adjoining taller buildings. Quaint, aged, and of an unusual colonial design, the house which dates from about 1660 gives promise of standing many years more.

CHURCH ONCE FIRED UPON BY AMERICAN "REBELS"

THE Brattle Square Church (Congregational-Unitarian) is an historic Boston landmark of Colonial days. Built in 1772 and demolished in 1871, it was located on the southwest corner of Brattle square, now the site of a clothing establishment. In 1775 it was conscripted by the British troops as a troop barracks and during street fighting was fired upon by the "rebels" of the city, one cannon ball striking the front of the building to the right of the window over the entrance (black spot). The cannon ball was saved and inserted where it struck.

THE OLDEST BOARDING SCHOOL IN AMERICA

IN this little red schoolhouse, on March 1, 1763, Master Samuel Moody heard the first recitation in an American boarding school. The sketch shows this original building of Governor Dummer Academy at South Byfield, which resulted from the thought of Lt.-Gov. William Dummer of the Mass. Bay Colony who left his attractive Byfield estate in trust to found a boy's boarding school.

Paul Revere made the school's seal. Edward Preble, Theophilus Parsons, Samuel Sewall, attended the school, and the names Adams, Choate, Frothingham, Hale, Longfellow, Cabot, Sargent, and Pickman are among those appearing often in the list of Master Samuel Moody's students.

PROMINENT BOSTONIAN GAVE SEX TO AN ENGLISH CATHEDRAL

A BOSTONIAN who enforced his opinion on Old England is William Deane Howells, whose home at 4 Louisburg square is the second house seen in the sketch. He described Wells Cathedral in Somerset as the feminine cathedral of England and his view has been generally accepted.

Boston has inherited much from London and borrowed much, but in this instance, at least, the tide of influence was reversed. Many guide books have incorporated Howells' idea and most people now look upon this great cathedral as feminine.

Such is the force of tradition that there seems nothing incongruous in attributing sex to a ship, but in the case of these impressive masses of stone it appears novel. It is not unique, however, for certain persons have maintained that Ely Cathedral is the only feminine cathedral in England.

HISTORIC HOUSE WITH SECRET PASSAGE . . .

THE Historic Winslow House Association, Inc., Arthur Winslow, President, and Lewis W. Hall, Treasurer, controls the destiny and welfare of the mansion built in 1699 by Hon. Isaac Winslow on the land and near the site of his grandfather's (Gov. Edward Winslow) and father's (Gov. Josiah Winslow) house which was burned. It is situated in Marshfield, Mass. Among those on the Board of Governors are Mr. William Sumner Appleton of the Society for the Preservation of New England Antiquities, and Miss Henrietta Hall of Marshfield Hill, Mass.

Among the many interesting architectural features of the interior is the secret passage to the attic, reached through the cupboard to the right of the tall fireplace in the South East chamber. Some other noteworthy bits are: the nearly perfect Jacobean stairway with fine paneling, acorn drops, heavy turned spindles and fat rail, all a beautiful snuff brown color common to unpainted or unoiled white pine; oddly built fireplaces throughout, not converging inward to a smaller back, but going in perfectly straight and touching the back with a semicircular curve; and a most interesting front hall, to which nothing was done during the restoration or remodelling of the house.

The house sheltered many masters, including Daniel Webster. Robert Prichard Eaton classed the landmark as representing two periods—"the original, the very late 17th century and the rather heavy Georgian period of 1756." There are but very few examples of the earlier period preserved in this country.

JACK FROST
1936

ALL EUROPE IN GREAT HALL ON BOSTON'S BEACON HILL

THIS room is the banquet hall of the Boston Architectural Club at 16 Somerset street, Boston. It is
made up of bits of architecture inspired by coun-
tries throughout Europe. The predominant features are
Elizabethan, however. There is hardly a country which
one could visit in Europe without finding some reminder
of it here in this high-beamed room.

Throughout the house are other many interesting architectural features. The baronial hall which one enters first
is most unusual.

ANCIENT CASTLE AND THE FIRST UNION FLAG

ON Oct. 29, 1903, Prospect Hill park, Somerville, Mass., with its fine observatory shown in the sketch, was dedicated. The Union flag with its 13 stars and stripes first bade defiance to an enemy Jan. 1, 1776, from the summit of Prospect Hill. In the following year the Continental Congress arranged for the flag of the United States, which except for stars in the blue field in place of the crosses of St. George and St. Andrew was quite similar to the flag which flew over Prospect Hill.

So, on the spot where floated the first Union flag stands a reproduction of a vari-styled old-time castle, designed and constructed by City Engineer Ernest W. Bailey. The city seal of Somerville shows Washington standing on this hill with a Union flag unfurled.

JACK FROST
1935

AN IMPORTANT BOSTON ACTOR BECAME INTOXICATED THROUGH A KEY HOLE.

A FAVORITE tradition of the stage has it that John Wilkes Booth, the murderer of Lincoln, whose home at 29A Chestnut street is shown in the sketch, had such a weakness for liquor that there was a constant danger that his roles would be wrecked by his appearance, drunk, before the footlights. Often to guarantee a sober performance, he was locked in his room, according to the tradition. Nevertheless, on one occasion in Boston, when the company called at his locked room to let him out for the show, he was deeply intoxicated, having bribed a servant to feed him spirits through the keyhole with the assistance of a straw. His brother, the great Edwin Booth, entered a saloon but once in his life—for the purpose of gambling. He lost $20.

THE SKELETON IN COSTUME

MANY mysteries are to be found in the history of the islands of Boston harbor. But none of them has proved more baffling than the mystery of the "skeleton in costume" found by workmen in 1905 when repairs were being made at Fort Independence on Castle Island.

The bones, still clothed in an ancient military costume, were found when an old casemate, long since sealed up with brick and mortar, was broken open.

Neither the identity of the soldier nor the explanation of his presence there has ever been determined, despite much research into official records and histories.

It is a curious coincidence that Edgar Allan Poe, who wrote "The Cask of Amontillado," one of the most famous of all short stories, was once stationed at this same fort when he was a young man, and that his well-known story was built around just such an incident.

JACK FROST
1935

DRUNKEN CHIMNEYS

NEITHER London nor Paris could produce more crazily leaning and eccentric chimneys than Marblehead, Mass. Here is an example of the sturdy independence and originality of the true New England character. Pictured is the rear of the King Hooper house at 8 Hooper street, Marblehead, which was built in 1745. Lopsided though they are, the chimneys are well constructed and seem to have a few more centuries of life in them.

OLD PILGRIM FORT BECOMES ATTRACTIVE HOUSE

TIMBERS hewed by the Pilgrims can be seen in the Harlow house in Plymouth, Mass., shown in the sketch. The house dates to 1677.

The building was formerly called the Water-Hole House, as there was a boggy hollow near it which has since been filled. When it was erected, beams and rafters from the old fort in Burial Hill were used in its con-struction, making it a valuable relic of the earliest days of Massachusetts history.

The graceful old house on Sandwich street is of inter-est because of its old-fashioned New England design as well as its historical importance. At the time of the ter-centenary celebration in Plymouth it was one of the centers of activity in the town. Each season the house attracts almost as many visitors as Plymouth Rock itself.

JACK FROST
1935

AN INDIAN RESERVATION ON BEACON HILL

AT the rear of 23 Chestnut street, Boston, is a colony of nine or ten Indians of various sizes—all members of the "wooden Indian" tribe. One is a true cigar store Indian, with a handful of stogies. Another shades his eyes with his hand and looks toward the horizon. Another leans heavily on a staff. It is probable that it is a valuable colony, since the demand for wooden Indians has increased greatly in recent years. They were collected by Wilmot Evans, and are now the property of his estate.

MAZE —
CEDAR HILL
WALTHAM

WALTHAM'S MAZE

THE maze at Cedar Hill, Waltham, Mass., shown in the sketch, is patterned on the famous maze at Hampton Court, England, but is constructed entirely of arbor vitae, while its English prototype has seven varieties of evergreens. It is situated on the Girl Scout's reservation of 85 acres.

The maze was created in 1897 by Miss Cornelia Lyman Warren, who died in 1922, as a center of attraction for children and holiday-seekers. She bequeathed portions of the estate, the old Warren farm at Cedar Hill, to the city of Waltham for park purposes, the Girl Scouts, Harvard and Massachusetts Institute of Technology.

The maze cost $50,000 and due to the slow growth of the shrubs it was not complete for seven years. It is 96 feet wide at the front and 226 at the rear and each of the sloping sides measures 115 feet 9 inches.

JACK FROST
1935

THE HOME OF THE TIMID TORY

IF Isaac Royall, the Tory, was timid, as his contemporaries of the early 18th century termed him, he also was generous, and his old mansion in Medford, Mass., is a sort of monument which has perpetuated his memory. He left the first legacy Harvard law school ever received, consisting of profits from local land.

In December, 1737, the "timid Tory" asked the General Court to remit a duty of four pounds a head on "a parcel of Negroes." He then contended that the slaves were intended for his own use, and not for merchandise. The old slave pens may still be seen. The Royall House Association maintains the dwelling, which was built at 15 George street in 1732.

GETTING AWAY FROM BULFINCH

THE chief glory of federalist Boston was the architecture of Bulfinch. It has been debated more than once whether he followed London or whether London followed him. Chronology favors Bulfinch. But his successors broke away from his style, producing in the end such classic structures as the customs house, which today hides the foundations of the 20th century tower. Chief among those architects after Bulfinch was Asher Benjamin, who built the old West Church in Chambers street, in the West End, Boston, about the time Bulfinch's new State House was going up. An examination of this building, especially its rounded window-tops, indicates that in 1806 Benjamin was still influenced by the master. The building is now a branch of the Boston Public Library. While still a church, it had as one of its pastors the father of James Russell Lowell.

"FAIR HARVARD" WAS WRITTEN IN RADCLIFFE COLLEGE

ALTHOUGH "Fair Harvard" was written by a Harvard man, the song which is a favorite at all Harvard commencements and football games found its place of birth in a room of what was the first Radcliffe College. That was Fay House, at 12 Garden street, Cambridge, where the Rev. Samuel Gilman put the song to paper.

When Fay House was built in 1807, it was known as "Ireland's Folly," because watchful neighbors considered it too ambitious a dwelling for its young owner, Nathaniel Ireland. He did indeed become very poor within a few years.

Fay House serves today as the administration building of Radcliffe. The architect drew his inspiration from Bulfinch. The most gracious room is the so-called President's room, typical of the early 18th century in every respect save the installation of a modern desk lamp.

THE DINKY HOUSE

ONE of the less widely known oddities of Beacon Hill, Boston, may be seen from Joy street. It is the "Dinky House." If you will look up the alleyway between the two restaurants near No. 36 Joy street, shown in this drawing, you will see a house so small that it seems destined for dolls. It may remind you of the small, stack-chimneyed, slope-roofed cottages that are found so often near village railroad stations in Maine. Like them, it makes up for what it lacks in size by the favor it has gained with those who know it. But even they have never called it anything but "the dinky house."

JACK FROST
1936

"BOSTON STUMP" IN TRINITY CHURCH

AS evidence of the bond that exists between Boston and its elder namesake in England is the tracery, or ornamental stone work, shown in the sketch, to be found at Trinity Church, whose rector is the Rev. Arthur Lee Kinsolving.

The elaborate design was taken from St. Botolph's Church in Boston, England, the tower of which is known locally as "the Boston Stump." The tracery, a characteristic of 14th century architecture, may be seen to the side of the rear of Trinity Church, facing on Clarendon street.

While Bostonians have raised funds to aid in restoring the ancient church abroad, a little of its old world beauty has been sent back across the Atlantic in return.

HARVARD STUDENTS AND CANNONBALLS FOR STOVES

IN those days when Harvard's reputation was in the process of becoming known to the world, many luxuries were lacking. In fact, a most humorous yet adequate method was used for heating the rooms of a cold night.

Possibly to save fuel, a cannon ball was used to radiate the heat. The ball was heated among the embers of the fireplace during the day, and when the flames sifted out at nightfall—and bedtime—it was placed in a brazier in the room. Then it threw its heat to the sleeping sons of Harvard, with no further cost of fuel, and no fire to watch.

One of these heating implements was dropped from a window to the steps beneath, and the break in the second step may be seen today, a material tribute to the thrift and ingenuity of a past day in the history of Harvard College. These are the steps to the left of Hollis hall which was built by the Province of Massachusetts Bay in 1763, and was used as barracks by the Colonial troops, 1775-76. It was named after a merchant of London, Thomas Hollis, and others members of his family, benefactors of the college.

HISTORIC HOUSE BOUGHT BY MAN FROM HIMSELF

AS has been said before, anything may be expected upon Beacon Hill in Boston, but we feel that when a man actually buys his own home, that is the last straw.

Two of Boston's most intelligent citizens deliberately bought their own houses. One, upon various occasions having SPOKEN about selling his estate, was dared one day by a broker to name a price. Piqued, the owner instantly stated $50,000 as his price. Appallingly, the other took him up on it, and the result was that he had to pay $10,000 to live in his own house, because one of his family was unwilling to move.

Another dweller of the Hill repented of a sale upon more logical consideration, and voluntarily rescinded the contract at the same cost. Because there was no change of title, he, therefore, purchased the house from himself. Both men lived upon Beacon street. The second dwelling shown in the sketch was once the home of William Prescott at 55 Beacon street.

PILOT HOUSE OF ROMANTIC TUG NOW A CANDY STORE

EVEN tugboats come to peculiar ends, and remarkable and interesting is the commercial use to which the pilot house of the old tug, Captain Drum, has been put. In a rugged setting of sails and masts, the sign-bedecked craft now rests near the art colony of Gloucester at Rocky Neck, Mass.

Many stories have been told of the tug Captain Drum, and many remark upon the ways of fate—that a powerful ship's pilot house should pass its last days as a "candy store." But this use at least preserves the cabin for observation, whereas if it were not converted to such use, it would probably have been destroyed long ago.

Jack Frost 1937

CONTRAST IN OLD BOSTON HOUSES

THIS sketch shows a contrast in houses. The lovely house in the foreground was that of Jeffrey Richardson and was built in 1796 at High and Pearl streets, Boston.

Later it became the Congress House, a hotel. The ornate structure at the rear was known as "Harris's folly." It was built in 1800 by Jonathan Harris, a merchant who made a great deal of money suddenly in one of Boston's early boom periods. He tried to establish an elaborate menage in the continental manner, but lived in the house only eight years before moving to more modest quarters. Another of the ornate residences of early Boston was known as "Eaton's folly" and was on Chambers street near Eaton street.

JACK FROST.

THE OLDEST HOUSE IN NEW ENGLAND

THE Indian race was still the most populous in Massachusetts when the Fairbanks house in Dedham was built, and no doubt the builders kept well-primed muskets close to their saws and axes while they worked. Apparently the structure went up soon after 1636, and through the centuries it has remained in possession of the Fairbanks family, which often has reunions there.

In a manner as pleasing to the eye as a well-chiselled piece of sculpture, the old homestead combines the double-sloped and the pitch roof. Although sturdy, the home looks its age, and so far as can be learned, it is entitled to classification as the oldest house in New England.

JACK FROST
1935

THE THRIFT OF BENJAMIN FRANKLIN

EVEN in his words was Benjamin Franklin thrifty. Perhaps one of the best examples of this fact is the almost spectacular conservatism of the inscription on the monument which he erected to his parents. The stone bears but one word—Franklin.

"Poor Richard" certainly had a lot he could have crammed into an epitaph; he loved his parents dearly. By nature conservative and wise, he also lived in an age quite different in spirit from the blatant modern times. The monument is in the Old Granary Burial Ground, Tremont street, Boston.

Jack Frost

HOUSE OF SEVEN GABLES HAS EIGHT GABLES

SALEM'S most popular place of romantic background is the House of The Seven Gables. At the foot of Turner street, Salem, Mass., it stands in all its quaintness, facing the water.

However, the house has at present eight gables, not counting the gabled door to the garden, and the owner, Miss Emmerton, maintains that before Hawthorne wrote of it there were also eight gables. One was evidently down at the time he was producing his famous story. Historically, there is a much tangled story as to the changing number of gables.

JACK FROST
1935 11

THE OLD HOWARD ROPED OFF EVERY TWENTY YEARS

IN about six years a part of the sidewalk in front of the Old Howard will be roped off, as it was in 1904 and on July 2, 1924, to keep the public from a small part of the pavement. In order to retain title to the land, the owners must declare their ownership every 20 years by displaying their right to a part of the sidewalk. Other-wise, the sidewalk would become public property by prescriptive right.

This is one of America's oldest theatres. Now used for burlesque, it contrasts oddly with its past. It has the only Shakespearian theatre construction still extant in this country.

MASSACHUSETTS' LOST UTOPIA

THE sketch of the above peaceful scene shows one of the most famous houses in Massachusetts. "Fruitlands" as it was called because fruit was to be the principal staple of daily food and to be cultivated on this farm wherein the Transcendentalists carried on their quest for peace, religion and happiness. Here came A. Bronson Alcott in 1843, and as an example of what the ideals and ideas of the colony was to be, planted the mulberry trees at the corner of the house, so that they might obtain silk from the silkworms placed there, with which to provide variety into the linen raiment of the community. It was one of their precepts that neither man nor beast should be sacrificed or deprived that others might exist.

Many famous personages were either associated with this experiment or visited their friends there who were. Henry Thoreau, Hawthorne and Emerson partook of the nuts, grain and fruit which constituted the diet of these members of the "Con-Sociate Family" here.

MEDIEVAL CASTLE ON GLOUCESTER SHORE

SOUVENIRS, modest or luxurious, from every country of Europe are among the treasures of the castle of John Hays Hammond, Jr., in Gloucester, Mass., and the whole structure seems typical of the beetling piles in which feudal barons once lived.

A drawbridge and its moat can even be seen on the inland side of the castle. Certainly, should Leif Ericson come out of the past and moor his Norse galleys on the Gloucester shore today he would feel quite at home. One of the many features of the modern chateau is an excellent art museum, owned by Mr. Hammond and regarded by him as fondly as some of his inventions.

YALE'S "SINGING TOWER" . . .

YALE UNIVERSITY in New Haven, Connecticut, abounds in attractive and unique bits of architecture. Even High street which passes through the College of Fine Arts has an interesting story. It passes under a picturesque arch which settled an argument. The University acquired land on either side of the thoroughfare and wished to close the road to traffic and erect a building across it. City officials objected to this and a compromise in the form of an arch connecting the Gallery with Street Hall at the corner of Chapel street resulted.

But Yale's crowning architectural glory is the deliciously graceful "singing Tower" on High street, erected in memory of Charles W. Harkness, class of '83. It casts an inspiring shadow over the University's 5,130 students, and adds magnificence to vistas from almost every part of the Memorial Quadrangle. Sketched above, this structure shows the influence of European models, particularly "the Boston Stump" in Boston, England, the frontispiece of this book. The Tour de Beurre of Rouen Cathedral also probably aided in the plans for the creation of the Yale edifice.

JACK FROST   1936

A FOUR-FOOT TREE 120 FEET HIGH IN DOWNTOWN BOSTON

HIGH up on Tremont Temple, Tremont street, Boston, rooted in a tiny crevice, is a small tree which can be seen from the street by those who take the trouble to look up. It has been growing several years, and clings so tenaciously to its airy perch that attempts to pull it out have been unsuccessful. Undoubtedly the seed from which it grew was carried to the crevice by a pigeon.

REVOLUTIONARY TAVERN, VAULT AND OLDEST SHOE STORE

THIS North End building seems to have almost as many historical attachments as bricks. Now a shoe store, and probably the oldest of its sort in America, the edifice at 10 Marshall street, Boston, early in its life knew the clinkings of steins and the mullings of old wine. It was a tavern then, with which were associated such figures as John Hancock, his uncle, Thomas, William Davenport, the brother-in-law of Benjamin Franklin, and Thomas Marshall. And, of course, Washington slept there.

In the lower rooms of this building were stored 2,000,-000 silver crowns, sent by France to help pay the colonial troops. This sum, about $250,000, was distributed by Ebenezer Hancock, deputy paymaster-general of the revolutionary army and youngest brother of John Hancock.

"WHITE CHURCH" HAS PAUL REVERE BELL

THE Second Church, Dorchester, Mass., shown in the sketch, was built in 1806 in Codman square, named for its first minister, the Rev. John Codman, D.D. There have been few alterations in the original Colonial structure.

The three original parishes in Dorchester were Unitarian, Congregational and Unitarian, in that order. Sixty families, remote from the parish, at Meetinghouse Hill, formed the congregation of the Second Church, Congregational. The big bell was one cast by Paul Revere. The church has always been known as the "white church" because it has never been painted any other color.

A modern parish house was built in 1924, but the church proper still contains its original hand-hewn timbers, 70 feet in length, which were floated down from the Penobscot river.

"THE HOUSE WHERE PLANS WERE LAID WHICH ENDED THE REVOLUTIONARY WAR"

THE house owned in 1781 by Joseph Webb, friend of George Washington, is shown in the sketch. It is now owned by the Connecticut Society of the Colonial Dames of America and stands on Main street, Wethersfield, Conn. It is probable that the military conference held in this house on May 22, 1781 was the most important of the American revolution. For at that time General Washington, with Count de Rochambeau, fixed the plan of the Campaign, which ended the War with the surrender of General Cornwallis at Yorktown, Va., October 19, 1781.

The importance of this conference is indicated by the appropriation by the Conn. General Assembly of 500 pounds, a considerable sum in 1781, to defray the expense "to be incurred in quartering **General Washington, General Knox, General Duportail, Count de Rochambeau, Count de Barras,** and the **Chevalier de Chastellux,** and their suites, in Wethersfield."

According to Washington's diary, a good deal of private conversation with Governor Trumbull, gave it that if any important offensive operations should be undertaken, there was little doubt of the General being able to obtain men and provisions adequate to his wants. In this Colonel Wadsworth and others concurred.